Riding Bicycles

by Michèle Dufresne

Literacy Footprints, Inc.

Riding a bicycle can be
lots of fun.
You can go many places
on your bicycle.
You can ride your bike fast, or
you can ride your bike slow.

You should wear a **helmet** every time you ride a bike. It will help keep you safe.

When you ride your bike,
you must follow the rules
of the road, just like drivers
in cars do.

When you ride your bike,
never ride out into the road
without looking both ways first.

Use hand **signals** to let drivers in cars know what you are doing.

stop

left turn

right turn

There are many kinds of bikes.

Here is a mountain bike. You can ride a mountain bike on unpaved roads and dirt trails.

This bike rides low to the ground.

This tandem bike is built for two riders.

This is a rickshaw. In some countries of the world, people pull things on the back of their bikes.

Some people do tricks with their bikes. Doing tricks can be very **dangerous**!

It takes many years to learn to do tricks safely.

Some people like to race
with their bikes.
Some bikes are made
just for racing.
It can be a lot of fun,
but lots of work, too!

Glossary

dangerous: full of risk; able or likely to do harm

helmet: a hard covering worn to protect the head

signals: hand or body movements used to communicate

Index